20'24 (a collection of 20 poems for the year '24)

Ayesha Aly Sultana

BookLeaf Publishing

India | USA | UK

Presentation by *BookLeaf Publishing*

Web: www.bookleafpub.com

E-mail: info@bookleafpub.com

ISBN: 9789360942335

First edition 2024

To Maa & Baba...

(the two halves of my DNA)

ACKNOWLEDGEMENT

I want to thank Allah the almighty!

And in humans—my husband, both of our parents, our families, my teachers, relatives, friends and every single person who has some role in my life. Last but not least, the publisher of the book.

Jazakallah khair!

PREFACE

The delightfully imperfect illustrations have
been lovingly created by the author!

The Art of Pleasing

Difficult is the art
of pleasing people
while being honest.
For honesty is harsh
and doesn't please the mass.
May I propose a better option?
Please the Creator,
not the creation.
As people may or may not like
your honesty,
whereas it is what is loved
by Almighty!

Fine Dine Fever

Posh! Posh! Posh!
It's money that talks.
Top notch! High end!
Fine dine rocks!
The food on my plate
is an art indeed!
Now a perfect click
is all I need!
The vibe of the place
and the colours on my plate
are a treat for my eyes indeed!
Click! Click! Click!
Few shots candid!
As I'm paying for the blobs,
smokes and dots,
paying for the crumbs and drops.
Those zigzag lines and
a spoon of foam,
dusted cocoa on a glop.
A slice of steak
on a splash of sauce

and a rosemary makes it pop.
A caramel nest on a
a dollop of cream
with an edible flower on top!
Now eat! eat! eat!
The fancy treat!
A spoonful morsel
and that's it?
Full course, last plate;
I'm not full yet.
Stomach still growling
Roar! Roar! Roar!
Outta budget,
can't ask for more!
"Here is your bill Sir,
cash or card?"
The moment of truth...
My heart! My heart!
Then the place I left
with an empty wallet
and an empty stomach too,
and a genuine question
I kept thinking:
what is the role of food?
The vibe was good.
It stood as it should.
But the role of food
is to feed I guess?
Garnishing otherwise...

does it make sense?
Michelin star
spent quality time
leaving kitchen counter
full of scraps,
to make a bite-size dish
that barely covers
one-third of a plate
to the max!
Whatever! Anyways!
It's been many days
I had a fever of fine dine.
Money went to trash bin;
I got my medicine!
Now my health is fine.
So enough of high-end!
Done with top-notch!
Now, let's head home
to the bowl of hotchpotch!

Puzzle

Life is a jigsaw puzzle
with specific blank space.
And only the right piece
can match the right place.
Indeed he was incredible,
but a wrong tile for your puzzle.
So don't force, let go...
shed tears, don't show.
(It's hard, I know.)
With time things heal
and better you feel.
So calm down, pray hard...
take time, restart.
The right fit, right tile
is somewhere meanwhile.
Have faith in fate.
Don't worry, just wait
for the right day, right date.
As everything is destined
and so... is... he...

and his timing
to come by thee.
So chin up and smile,
he is on his way—
to come complete your puzzle
and take you away!

Mica Mines

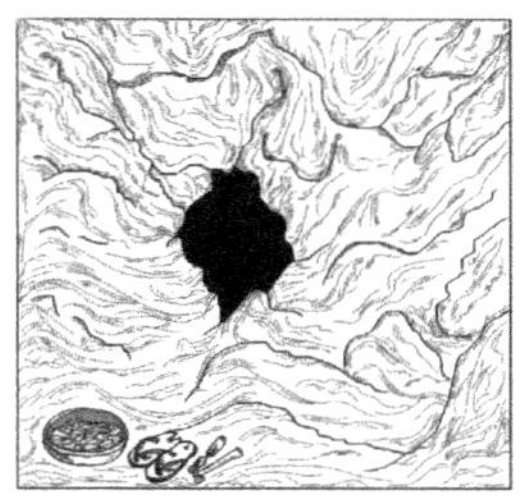

Mica the mined mineral
in your eye-shadow
or make-up in general.
The reason behind the
shimmer, the sparkle!
Safe on skin,
indeed natural!
But perhaps sourced
in ways unethical.
Are your products
cruelty-free for real?
Even if it's not tested
on animals,
but is child labour
less cruel?
Read ingredients,
question brands
about unsafe mines,
and bruised hands
that pick mica flakes

for half a dollar a day
or even less.
The men, the women,
their tender tween children...
all are risking their lives
in those illegal mines,
that glitter and shine
(having no other option).
For hunger ignores the caution!
10-20 deaths a month
in mine collapse.
Or even more, perhaps!
Is it worth your
pearlescent glow?
There has to be an ethical way
of mining for sure.
A way to provide fair wage
and safety for the chore.
A way to uproot child labour
from the core.
A way for the children to
go to school, play more.
And the change starts with you.
Ask the brands you use—
to be more transparent,
to be more see-through!

Sharp Edges

Yes!
The words you say
have sharp edges...
enough to bleed
my heart, I guess.

And then, a "sorry"
from your side...
and you think
you cleaned the mess?

Then you take back
the words you said,
like taking back
the sword you slayed.
The damage is done,
nevertheless.

And with time
shall heal the heart...
until the time
again you start,
like a loop
with no end...
until the dent
is permanent!

Yes!
Be a little less
careless...
when using words
with sharp edges!

EncyCROWpedia

More or less we all know,
the story of the thirsty crow.
In the story, we witnessed
the bird's intelligence.
With the brain size as small as a nut,
how come they are as smart
as a child aged seven or so?
Let's talk more about the Crow.

Genus Corvus has many species.
Crows, ravens... common are these.
All are broadly known as crow,
and there's so much about them to know.
Like: they have their own dialect to talk,
they hold grudges, they even stalk.
Good learners, problem solvers,
but at times they are mischievous.
They are of different sizes and shapes,
they are known as feathered apes.
20 years is their average lifespan.
And they are very loyal to their clan.

They even know how to make their tools!
Very smart, yet at times fools.
As cuckoos laid their eggs
smartly in their nests.
They pull the wool over their eyes
and outsmart the very wise.
Anyway,
they keep our city clean
by feeding on the garbage bin.
When one finds something to eat,
he calls the entire gang for the treat.
Young crows babysit their siblings too,
isn't that really cute?
They love open areas with trees,
but they don't migrate overseas.
They don't forget a face.
If you mess with them,
they will surely chase.
If one dies, they all gather
to find the predator
and to hold a funeral,
or just to mourn in general.
Like they hold grudges,
they hold gratitude too.
If you show them mercy,
they might bring gifts for you.

For a fact, I know,
"Bird-brain" can't be an insult

if the brain is of a crow.
But after all their cleverness,
helpfulness, cleanliness...
they're considered unlucky instead.
They have been labelled "the omens of death!"
Crows are portrayed in a negative light.
Is it because they are black, not white?
Or is there any other reason?
Perhaps, just another superstition.
When many crows are seen together,
their group is called a "murder!"
Why do we call them that?
Isn't it really sad?
Aren't they scavengers of the sky?
Can their help to mankind be denied?
Then why on their name,
there is so much dirt?
Why can't we treat them
like any... other... bird?

Candyfloss

Like a colourful candyfloss,
I entered in your life.
Little did I know,
you were a bowl of water!

The story ended
as soon as it began.
You swallowed my life out
and took my colour away.
Now your life is colourful,
but mine... rests in peace.

Autobiography

What date is today?
Check.
It's the first and last date of its kind.
For no two dates are the same.
Every day is like a new fresh page
with page number that denotes
how long have you been here.
Some pages you write well,
some you leave blank,
some you write fast,
and some pretty slow...
some pages with good handwriting,
and some like a child's scribble.
Some pages you write like never before,
that page becomes memorable.
Some pages you write the worst,
that page haunts you forever.
You get a new page,
a new beginning every day!
Every day is a restart.

So write, keep writing.
Write the new page
better than the previous one.
It's ok if you haven't covered the full page,
as long as your writings are meaningful.
But remember—
once a page is turned over,
that certain numbered page is gone forever.
You can't go back, edit or tear the page.
Once written, you can't erase anything—
not even a dot!
So... write carefully!
Don't write anything you'll regret.
But we are humans and we make mistakes.
So, learn from them and correct in the
coming pages and never repeat.
Write mindfully, write from heart,
write giving cent percent of all you have.
For pages are limited
and extra sheets are not provided.

Days will pass and pages will lessen,
countdown will come to an end.
And one day your book will be complete.
That day is your last day on earth,
and that book you wrote my friend—
is your actual autobiography!
Make it worth reading.
Cover to cover!

The Death Talk

Digits keep changing
every year.
Freeze my age,
death is near.

Wrinkles, grey hair...
I don't like.
Where can I buy
elixir of life?

Hear me out
oh my Dear,
eternal life
is not here!

No matter how
scared you feel,
no matter how many
times you appeal,
every soul will taste death—

it is the truth!
And it is the deal.

Digits keep changing,
so do you.
Change is the constant,
all go through.
So like the old you,
embrace the new.
Ageing is beautiful,
and so are you!

And death has nothing
to do with age.
You can be young,
you can be old,
you can be newborn
on last page.

Don't be scared.
Death is not end
but a door to infinity,
my dear friend.
You will get there,
here what you seed!
so don't stress on death—
but on good deed!

Finding Myself

I have lost myself
while trying to fit in
the human crowd.
All I gained but,
a severe self-doubt.
To cater to different people,
I invented different
shades of mine.
In the process but,
I lost my true colour,
I lost my shine.
I forgot my values,
I forgot who I was.
I tried my best to
hide my flaws.
While striving to

win people's hearts,
I ignored my own.
All I wanted was
not to be left alone!
I tried my best
and it was tough.
For people,
I was never enough.
I corrupted my soul,
I changed me whole.
Acting and pretending,
I became a fake.
Losing authenticity
was a big mistake!
I have failed myself
while passing the
expectations of others.
I don't know the art
of saying "no"
when line is crossed
by people I know
(or hardly know).
I have become water—
no taste, no colour.
Some adding salt,
some pouring sugar.
I lost my transparency,
no wonder!
I buttered them

to get validation,
I buttered them
for I feared rejection.
But after all my efforts,
I'm still sitting alone
staring at the screen
of my phone.
I'm running out of butter,
I'm running out of peace.
Where are they
in my times of need?
On the other hand,
I'm scared to face myself,
I'm scared of the silence.
(For it asks valid questions
about my existence.)
I've long lost myself.
I'm craving me now.
All I want is,
my inner peace (somehow)!
I want to learn my worth.
I'm not here to entertain.
For it's my life,
where they have side roles
and I am the main!
Following heart isn't enough.
For a change,
I need to use my brain.
I should be my priority

to keep me sane.
I have to remind myself—
I was created by The Creator,
The Lord of the worlds.
Then why should I cheese people?
This is insane!
For the sake
of my inner peace,
I better turn to Him again!

One of a Kind Beautiful

You and I come from
the same Creator.
And all the faces that are
considered beautiful,
(by the so-called beauty standards)
are also from the same Creator.
Hence, same pinch!

He is the best of the designers.
He is the Designer of the designers.
And He designed me.
Hence, I am a designer piece.

He never makes mistakes.
And He purposely chose this body
to put my soul in.
Hence, I am not a mistake.

Perfection is for Him.
And He perfected me
with imperfections.

Hence, I am imperfectly perfect.

Since He does not use any mold,
every piece is unique.
Hence, I am one of a kind.

I am beautiful.
I am one of a kind beautiful.
I am a creation of The Creator.
Hence, you judging my look
is you judging His creation—
Do it at your own risk.

May I have Your Attention Please

"May I have your attention please..."
my attentive ears heard the call,
while sipping tea by the stall.
The station clock: 8:09.
I proceeded towards the yellow line.
Eyes on track, luggage in hand,
behind the line as I stand.
Arrived the train with a squeal sound.
People running, chaos around.
Stopped the train, I found my coach.
Towards my seat then I approached:
side lower berth 2B/65,
luggage placed, let's begin the ride!
All the new faces around me,
It feels very happy to see.
And then starts the train,
slow to fast again.
I'm eager to watch the window show,
while talking to people I hardly know.

Then come hawkers with delish food,
typical trade-cry lights the mood.
Through window watching live-telecast,
Discovery channel running fast.
Stations come and stations go,
I read the names so and so.
The landscapes keep throbbing heart,
I praise the Almighty for the stunning art!
Random people, random talk:
family, politics, market-stock...
In the corner cries a random kid,
coughs a man in the other seat.
Every time this blows my mind—
how various people of various kinds,
from different places having different goals,
were destined to be on one board!

Then at night, when all crash out,
looks like berths are carrying shrouds.
Then closing my eyes I swing, I sway.
The rhythmic shakes take me away.
The screeching noise, the hissing sound...
the train tunes hold me spellbound.
Every time someone opens the door,
the sound, the noise increases more.
Everything is worth falling in love.
The train journeys are never enough!
Next morning, the station is about to come.
Buh-bye strangers! My eyes are numb.

We meet once and never meet again.
How to explain this parting pain?
Our first... perhaps last meeting as well,
but they will reside in my memory cell.
The train slows down, it's time to leave.
They smiled at me, I started to grieve.
I smiled back with a heavy chest,
wishing them all the best.
Here we are... the home-station!
Finally reached my destination.
Tired me craving a cup of tea,
when I heard:
"May I have your attention please..."

Things would be Different

And one fine day
if you wake up with some tools
in your hand,
with a user manual
for you to understand.

Things would be different!

Like a pair of glasses to read
their intentions and detect their lies.
And a box of litmus paper
to test whether the tears are
true or crocodile's.

Things would be different!

And a CCTV that will
trace and track—
whoever, wherever, whatever
they talk behind your back.

Things would be different!

And a typewriter that types
the thoughts sitting in their brain
and feelings lying in their heart,
to align with the words
coming from their mouth.
(Is it in harmony or worlds apart?)

Things would be different!

But, not necessarily better!
For most of your relations (if not all),
will start to scatter
in left, right and centre.

His Handmade Paper

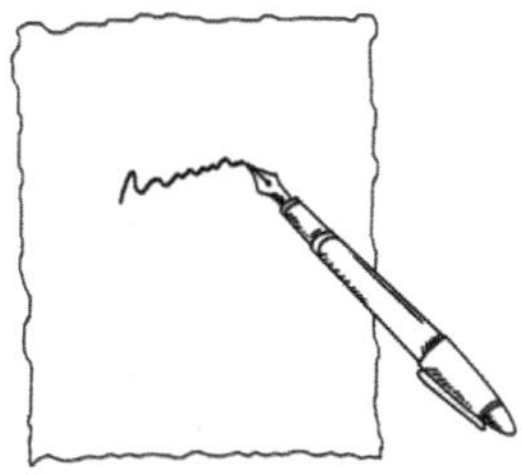

He tore the darkest page of her diary,
and shredded that in his paper shredder.
Then he filled a container with some empathy,
and patiently soaked the shredded paper in it.
Then he put it in a blender with some loyalty
and trust.
Then he put the pulp in a tub of water and
sprinkled some honesty,
followed by a passionate stir.
He then dipped his mold and deckle and lifted it
with utmost care.
He gave it a quick shake to drain out the tears.
Then gently removed the deckle,
and flipped the mold on a cosy towel like a
gentleman.
With a sponge, he started soaking all the pain
and traumas.
Then he lifted the mold with excitement.
The fragile sheet now has a shape;
he felt confident.

Then he dried the sheet
in the warmth of his love,
and compressed it with a tight hug.
He held the new paper with joy
and contentment,
and he kissed it all over.
"Your page is fresh, renewed, my dear.
Write again without any fear!"
Her eyes became glittery.
She took the page with a bashful smile.
He gave her a pen.
She held the pen firmly,
and—
wrote his name.

I am on The Way

I'm not in my distilled version yet.
I'm in the process everyday.
I fail but I try
and I go all the way.

It's hard I know
and I won't run away.
One step at a time,
moving slowly but moving,
and I am on the way.

I know I am out
on display.
I'm very cautious
of what I do or say.
But still,
get judged anyway!

Long left my
prototype version,
and development is
underway.
For I started as a flower,
slowly turning
into a bouquet.

The world is a stage.
In it, I have a character
to play.
I have good, I have bad;
I have both in fray.
I try for my goodness
to far outweigh.

How hard is
the right path!
And how easy is
to go astray!
May my Lord guide me,
by my side may He stay.

Before We Join a Tableau

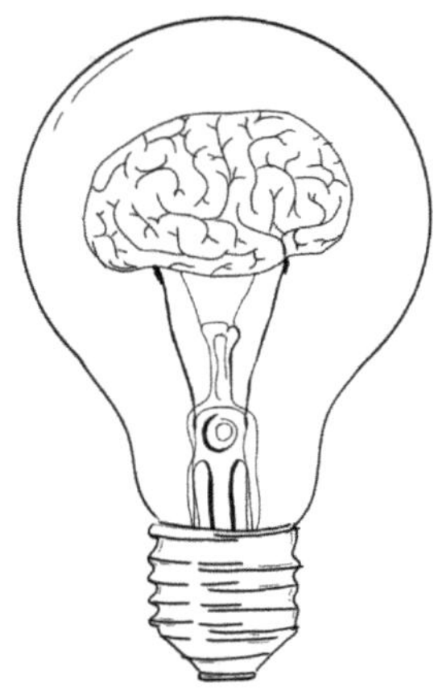

They have gathered a crowd;
their game is strong,
so nobody cares if
they are right or wrong.
We love to jump on bandwagon.
We fear to stand alone.
We love to be in the crowd,
for it makes us feel proud.
We love to be on the winning team.
We don't think before we scream.
We love to celebrate success,
even if it's fragile and hollow.
It's not the cause,
but the crowd we follow.
We have stopped thinking;

all we care about is what's trending.
But we forget,
whatever is trending today
might not trend tomorrow.
For trends come with an expiry date.
Think before it's too late!
But,
not all crowds are same;
not all voices are noise.
It's us who choose
either colony of bees,
or swarm of flies.
You will be amazed to know—
all of us have a brain!
For a change, let's use it
before we join a tableau!

Dear Well-wisher

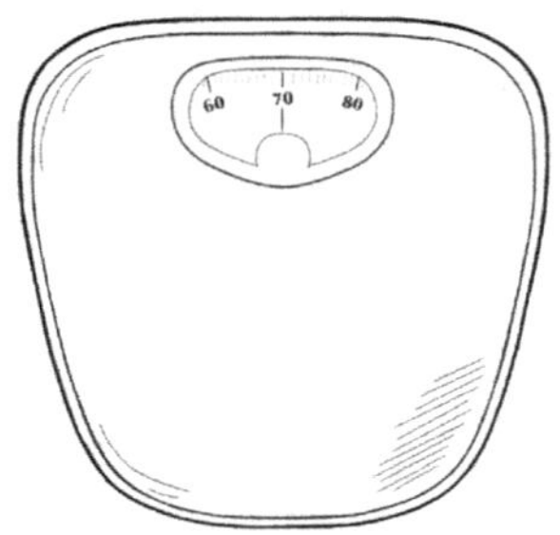

Thanks for always letting me know,
I'm fat.
(I don't own a mirror!)
Thanks for comparing me
with big objects.
I feel better!
Thanks for cracking those unfunny
fat jokes.
You're a true motivator!
Thanks for always trying to suck
my confidence out,
dear well-wisher!
Now that I know I'm big—
unlike your heart,
so even if I lose weight,
I still can't beat
the thin and narrowness
of your mind,
right?

You, Me and Punctuation

Dear, when you talk,
feel free to use
any punctuation
but full stop!

For, when you talk,
I go speechless—
all I can think of
is a line of ellipsis...

Your charming words
with exclamation mark
amaze me!
Your eyes glitter
everytime when
you praise me!

And the way
you are all ears
when I speak...
be it the important bits
that make sense
or simply the ones
(in parentheses)!

And when your colon-like eyes
switch to semicolon
for a fleeting wink.
You make my heart
skip a beat
and eyes forget to blink.

I do want you to retain
possession on me,
like a word is owned
by its previous word
with apostrophe.

And if you need a break,
I am up for a comma,
but don't you dare
give me the trauma
of a period.

Yes, I asked this
on purpose:

"Is there a question mark
about us?"
And I loved the
way you said:
"You are the
answer to my prayers."

"But, what if you find
someone just like me?"
You replied:
"Hyphens and dashes
may look alike
but can they be
used as alternatives?
They can never be!"

From my stupid questions
to your solid answers,
from the day
we came under
one quotation—
"You" and "Me"
became an "Us",
and it is ever thus!

Bon Appétit

Don't worry
if life looks like a mess.
See, flour can not turn into bread
until it's kneaded,
and the kneading process is indeed messy!
And if you give up in the middle of the process
(because it's messy),
you'll neither get bread
nor get the flour back.
Moreover, your hands will remain messy.
But, if you could trust the process and
continue kneading (ignoring the messiness),
soon you'll get a dough,
and your hands will be mess-free!
But wait, you didn't get the bread yet.
For that, the dough has to be taken out
of its comfort zone,
and exposed to the harshness of the oven.
The world is no less than an oven.
And if you too are exposed to its harshness—

congratulations!
You are just a step away from freshly baked
bread!
Bon appétit in advance!

Paying Them Back

Their entire world is around me,
but in my world they are nowhere.
The sacrifices they made for me,
should I really care?
Who forgot their dreams
to fulfil mine,
now I don't need their blessings,
as I am doing fine.
I might be the apple of their eyes,
but they are my eyesore.
In my priorities,
they don't exist anymore!

Who taught me how to behave,
now I misbehave with them.
Who carried me to my school,
now I try to school them.
Who taught me how to talk,

now I find it OK
to talk back to them.
Who held my fingers when I was little,
now I point my finger at them.
The voice that used to sing lullaby for me,
now I raise my voice to silence them!

Who spent restless nights
when I was sick,
I forgot their support
in my thin and thick.
I find their love and care annoying,
irritating their advice.
Who always wiped my tears away,
now I bring tears to their eyes!

Whose house was the safest place,
whose laps were the safest beds,
let alone those nine months in her womb
and each drop of milk I consumed.
Is old-age-home not a good return gift?—
It is! I presume.
Then why do people say:
they can never pay back their parents?
Look at me paying them back,
paying them back
with added interest!